Testimonials

We feature a link to the book on two of the national military organizations I work with and we have provided free copies to our members at our annual reunions. This book has been a wonderful resource for veterans, and you provide a great service to our nation and its veterans when you provide these free copies. Trying to navigate the VA system without professional help and information is difficult, frustrating and generally less successful. Please keep up this very, very important work.

Bill Dozier, MSGT USMC (RET)
Master Mason, Prince Hall Shriner
Secretary, Military Friends of Distinction
Member, Black Marine Reunion

I have read *The Road to VA Compensation Benefits* by Matthew Hill. It is a magnificent tool that every veteran should have. It is more than a book. It is a road map to guide veterans through the maze and sometimes confusing VA claim process for service related disability benefits. All of my clients who have had the opportunity of reading it have found it to be very helpful. It is a must read by all veterans, especially by those veterans who are dealing with disabilities they incurred during their time of service. Many thanks to Hill and Ponton for taking the time to produce this road map for those who have put their lives on the line for our freedom.

Pierre Saint-Fleur, PhD, DBA
Vet Center Director, Fresno Vet Center
1320 E. Shaw, Suite 125
Fresno, CA 93791
(559) 487-5660

Thank you for sending *The Road to VA Compensation Benefits* by Matthew Hill. I found it informative and helpful. I tell veterans to contact Hill and Ponton.

Michael Magyar
E-4 U.S. Army

I started my original claim three years ago in January. I had no idea of the amount of supportive materials needed and the process of submitting all the materials. If I would have known about your book and website (and the important thing – read and learn) it would have certainly got me off to a much better start and understanding of the system. I have had three C&P exams, and with no knowledge of preparation for the first one (heart stint), though I did get a rating, it could have been higher if I would how to prepare. So by my third C&P exam for PTSD, I was much more prepared and as well discovered your book and website. As the exam began it was like going down a check list of the questions that were being asked and I had appropriate answers for each in detail. It resulted in a 100% rating, that pleased me beyond measure. All this to say, so many Veterans could help themselves if they took time to study and prepare for their claims and C&P exams. My initial thoughts were that once you submitted your papers and filed the claim, that was pretty much it. So from my experience, I preach to Vets filing claims how important documentation and preparation are to get things right at the beginning, saving a lot headaches and lost time.

Ken Arbuckle

Special Thanks to

Sara Kathryn Hill

Important Disclaimer

This book does not offer legal advice. We provide background information about the VA claims process and what you can expect. If you have already retained an attorney or agent for your VA claim, please discuss the specifics of your case with them.

This book provides information about the VA claims process broken down into simple terms. For more in depth information about specific VA rules and regulations, please visit the blog on our website www.hillandponton.com.

Table of Contents

Introduction

Compensation benefits for our disabled veterans and their families have always received great support from the American public. This book walks through the process of filing a disability claim with the U.S. Department of Veterans' Affairs (VA).

There are many types of benefits for veterans and their family members, yet this book focuses solely on claims for service connected disability compensation handled by the Veterans Benefits Administration.

There are approximately 3.4 million veterans receiving VA compensation benefits. These benefits are intended to compensate for a veteran's average impairment in earning capacity caused by the disability. In other words, the less a veteran can work due to a service connected disability, the higher the veteran's rating should be. There are no income or asset limitations for entitlement to these benefits.

Unlike disability benefits paid by the Social Security Administration, total disability or entitlement to a 100% disability evaluation is not required for a veteran to receive service connected benefits. Moreover, the establishment of service connection, even at a 0% evaluation, may entitle a veteran to many non-compensatory benefits. These may include preference in federal/state employment, job retention rights, and basic entitlement to VA health care. These benefits are not considered taxable income and are not taxed by federal or state governments.

One of the biggest challenges a veteran faces is the long wait. The average wait time for a VA disability claim to be adjudicated is two to four years. Although there is very little that may be done to speed up this process, we hope to empower you with the knowledge you need to navigate the journey to service connected compensation.

Who Can File a Claim for Service Connected Disability Benefits?

As discussed before, this book focuses on a veteran's service connected disability claim. While some veterans' survivors are also eligible to file a claim, we will concentrate on an individual veteran's disability compensation claim. In order to file a claim for service connected disability compensation, there are multiple requirements.

First, you have to be a veteran. A veteran is a person that had active duty service in the military, naval or air services. Service in the various military academies or attendance in a military preparatory school may also qualify.

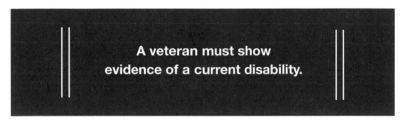

A veteran must show
evidence of a current disability.

Second, your discharge or separation from service must be undor conditions other than dishonorable. There is an exception for veterans who were discharged for committing certain offences but who were insane at the time of the offense. In these circumstances, the issue of insanity is determined by the VA.

Third, you must have a current disabling condition that can be linked to a disease, injury, or event in service. Specifically, the VA requires evidence that you have a disability on the date you

file the claim for benefits, or at another point during the length of your claim.

There has to be medical evidence of a current disability in order to meet this requirement. The evidence cannot be from a past disability that has ended. It is necessary to submit competent medical evidence that shows a presently existing condition or that the condition existed at some point since you filed the claim.

Furthermore, the in-service disease, event or injury must have occurred "in the line of duty." This means anything that occurred during the period beginning with induction and ending with discharge from military service. In fact, the Courts have stated that for the purposes of service connected compensation, a service member's day never ends. "In the line of duty," then, includes events that occur while you are on leave or off base. There is a caveat: service connection related to an in-service event may be granted only when the disability was not the result of the veteran's willful misconduct or the result of alcohol or drug abuse. Alcohol and drug abuse will be discussed later in greater detail.

Evidence Needed to Support Direct Service Connection

When filing a claim for service connection, you must provide the following to the VA:

(1) evidence of your current disability;

(2) evidence of your in-service disease, injury or event; and

(3) a medical statement that it is "as likely as not" that your current disability is related to service ("nexus" statement).

Provide evidence of your current diagnosis through your VA or private medical records. If you receive medical care at a VA medical facility, you may obtain copies of those medical records by submitting a VA Form 10-5345 directly to the Release of Information officer at the VA medical facility.

A statement describing your current symptoms is further evidence of your condition.

The key is to provide as much detail as possible regarding (1) the severity of the symptom, (2) how often you experience the symptom, and (3) for how long a period of time you have experienced the symptom.

Furthermore, evidence of your in-service event, disease, or injury may include service records, service medical records, and buddy statements. Buddy statements are sworn statements that can

describe an event in service. In some circumstances, they may be sufficient to support your claim.

For example, consider a veteran who claims service connection for Parkinson's Disease due to exposure to TCE in service. None of his service records document his TCE exposure. Yet, his service buddy writes a statement about how they cleaned weapons with a solvent that included TCE. This statement may help to prove the veteran's in-service event of TCE exposure.

Finally, to prove your claim for service connection, you need a nexus statement that links your current disability to the in-service event, injury or disease. In general, this statement must be made by a medical professional who concludes that it is "as likely as not" (50/50) that your current disability is related to service. The written medical opinion must also provide a rationale for the conclusion. Without a reasoned analysis, the VA will dismiss the medical opinion as unfounded.

Importantly, the VA is required by law to make reasonable efforts to assist you in obtaining evidence necessary to substantiate your claim. This evidence may include, for example, service records, service medical records, VA medical records, and private medical records.

If you would like the VA to obtain records for you, you must adequately identify the records and authorize the VA to obtain them.

Other Avenues to Service Connection

Above we discussed establishing service connection for conditions that are related to service in a direct way (occurring in service). Yet, there are several other ways a veteran may establish that a disability is service connected. Specifically, a veteran may establish service connection for a disability that::

   (1) was caused or aggravated by a service connected condition—this is referred to as secondary service connection;

   (2) existed prior to service and was aggravated or worsened during service—this is referred to as service connection by aggravation;

> Chronic conditions may change from mild to severe at times, but they never completely go away. They are permanent. The VA's list of chronic conditions includes arthritis, diabetes mellitus, schizophrenia, lupus, and multiple sclerosis.

(3) did not start in service, but is presumed to be connected to service based on a VA regulation—this is referred to as presumptive service connection. Presumptive service connection means that the veteran does not have to prove a connection between the condition and service to receive compensation.

Secondary Service Connection

The VA may grant service connection if the evidence establishes that it is as likely as not that the veteran's otherwise non-service connected disability was caused or aggravated by an already service connected disability.

For example, consider a veteran who is service connected for an ankle injury and develops a limp which causes back problems. This veteran can receive secondary service connection for the back problem if the medical evidence establishes that the back problem is as likely as not caused by the gait abnormality.

Service Connection by Aggravation

Even if a veteran has a condition which pre-existed service, that disability may still be deemed service connected if it is aggravated during the veteran's service. If a pre-existing condition worsens during service, the condition will be presumed to have been aggravated by service. For example, consider a veteran who suffered from ulcers prior to his enlistment. If his ulcers worsen during service, then he is entitled to compensation for the aggravation (worsening) of his ulcers.

Presumptive Service Connection for Conditions Related to Agent Orange Exposure

Certain diseases are presumed service connected for veterans who were exposed to Agent Orange. There are two parts to the VA's Agent Orange presumption. First, VA will presume that any veteran who stepped on the landmass of the Republic of Vietnam

Veterans who served in Vietnam were presumed to have been exposed to Agent Orange.

or served on the inland waterways was exposed to Agent Orange. Second, once the Agent Orange exposure is conceded, if the veteran develops any diseases on the list of those presumed to be caused by Agent Orange, that disease will be presumed to be service connected. The VA maintains a list of diseases that presumptive. Currently those diseases are:

AL amyloidosis
Chloracne or other acneform disease consistent
    with chloracne
Type 2 diabetes (also known as Type II diabetes mellitus
    or adult-onset diabetes)
Hodgkin's disease
Ischemic heart disease (including, but not limited
    to, acute, subacute, and old myocardial
    infarction; atherosclerotic cardiovascular disease
    including coronary artery disease
    (including coronary spasm) and coronary

bypass surgery; and stable, unstable and
Prinzmetal's angina)
All chronic B-cell leukemias (including, but not limited
to, hairy-cell leukemia and chronic lymphocytic
leukemia)
Multiple myeloma
Non-Hodgkin's lymphoma
Parkinson's disease
Early-onset peripheral neuropathy
Porphyria cutanea tarda
Prostate cancer
Respiratory cancers (cancer of the lung, bronchus,
larynx, or trachea)
Soft-tissue sarcoma (other than osteosarcoma,
chondrosarcoma, Kaposi's sarcoma, or
mesothelioma)

Note 1: The term "soft-tissue sarcoma" includes the
following:

Adult fibrosarcoma
Dermatofibrosarcoma protuberans
Malignant fibrous histiocytoma
Liposarcoma
Leiomyosarcoma
Epithelioid leiomyosarcoma (malignant
leiomyoblastoma)
Rhabdomyosarcoma
Ectomesenchymoma

Angiosarcoma (hemangiosarcoma and
    lymphangiosarcoma)
Proliferating (systemic) angioendotheliomatosis
Malignant glomus tumor
Malignant hemangiopericytoma
Synovial sarcoma (malignant synovioma)
Malignant giant cell tumor of tendon sheath
Malignant schwannoma, including malignant
    schwannoma with rhabdomyoblastic
    differentiation (malignant Triton tumor),
    glandular and epithelioid malignant
    schwannomas
Malignant mesenchymoma
Malignant granular cell tumor
Alveolar soft part sarcoma
Epithelioid sarcoma
Clear cell sarcoma of tendons and aponeuroses
Extraskeletal Ewing's sarcoma
Congenital and infantile fibrosarcoma

This list is constantly being updated and it is important to check with the regulation—38 CFR § 3.309 (e)—itself or hillandponton.com.

Even if a veteran did not serve in Vietnam, he can still get service compensation for a disease caused by Agent Orange. The VA acknowledges that the herbicide was used in other locations, such as the DMZ in Korea and the perimeter of USAF bases in Thailand during the Vietnam War. If the veteran did not serve in an area where the VA concedes that Agent Orange was used

then the veteran has to prove exposure through direct service connection. Hill & Ponton has been successful with these kinds of cases in Subic Bay but the burden to prove them is very high.

If the veteran was exposed to Agent Orange but did not develop a disease on the presumptive list, the veteran could still prove his case through direct service connection. The veteran will need a strong independent medical exam establishing that the condition was caused by the exposure. Hill & Ponton has been successful in this situation in cases such as kidney disease, hypertension, non-presumptive leukemias and Parkinson-like disabilities.

Presumptive Service Connection for Chronic Conditions

Additionally, presumptive service connection is available for diseases that are recognized by the VA as chronic. Chronic conditions may change from mild to severe at times, but they never completely go away. The VA's list of chronic—meaning permanent—diseases includes arthritis, diabetes mellitus, schizophrenia, lupus, and multiple sclerosis (MS), among others. The entire list may be found at 38 CFR § 3.309(a).

> **Chronic conditions can be granted presumptive service connection even if the condition never manifests in service. It just has to become active during the presumptive period.**

These chronic conditions are granted presumptive service connection only if they arose within an applicable time limit (presumptive period) after service, even if they did not arise specifically during service. The presumptive period for these conditions is generally one year following service, with a few exceptions, such as MS which has a seven-year presumptive period.

For example, consider a veteran who is diagnosed with lupus within one year of discharge, the presumptive period for lupus.

Following his diagnosis, he suffers no symptoms, receives no treatment and does not file a claim. If, years later, his lupus comes out of remission and he files a claim, the lupus will be service connected because it began during the appropriate presumptive period.

Consider another veteran who experiences ocular disturbances and lower extremity numbness during the first seven years after his discharge. No official diagnosis is made. Finally, ten years after service, testing indicates a diagnosis of MS. If a physician is able to provide a medical opinion that the symptoms he experienced within those first seven years (the presumptive period for MS) were in fact the early manifestations of MS, then his MS should be service connected.

Presumptive Service Connection for Conditions Related to Persian Gulf Service

The VA also offers presumptive service connection for certain conditions related to service in the Persian Gulf.

Veterans who served in Southwest Asia from August 1990 through the present, in operations such as Desert Shield, Desert Storm, Iraqi Freedom, and New Dawn, may qualify for presumptive service connection for certain illnesses.

These veterans may have been exposed to a wide range of environmental hazards that can contribute to the development of

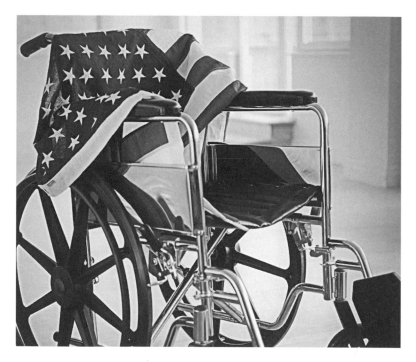

> **The VA recognizes that veterans who served in Southwest Asia were most likely exposed to environmental hazards such as smoke from oil well fires, solvent and fuel fumes, and contaminated food and water.**

diverse illnesses. These environmental exposures may include smoke from oil well fires, solvent and fuel fumes, pesticides, contaminated food and water, and air pollutants.

The VA recognizes that these exposures may lead to two medical outcomes. One outcome is referred to as an "undiagnosed illness." This means that a physician cannot diagnose the condition.

The other outcome is described as a "diagnosed medically unexplained chronic multi-symptom illness." This means that the illness can be labeled with a diagnosis, but its cause is not known. Examples of a chronic multi-symptom illness include chronic fatigue syndrome, fibromyalgia, and irritable bowel syndrome.

Signs and symptoms of these undiagnosed or unexplained illnesses include fatigue, skin rash, headaches, muscle pain, joint pain, indigestion, insomnia, dizziness, respiratory disorders, abnormal weight loss, impaired concentration, forgetfulness, and menstrual disorders.

These illnesses do not need to have started during service to be service connected. In fact, they can be compensated if they begin any time prior to December 31, 2016 (the current deadline stated in the VA regulations).

In addition to the illnesses outlined above, the VA presumes service connection for nine infectious diseases that are prevalent in Southwest Asia. These diseases are known to cause adverse long-term health effects.

To qualify for the infectious disease presumption, a veteran must have served in Southwest Asia during the Persian Gulf War, or must have served on or after September 19, 2001 in Afghanistan.

The qualifying diseases are brucellosis, campylobacter jejuni, coxiella burnetii (Q fever), malaria, mycobacterium tuberculosis, nontyphoid salmonella, shigella, visceral leishmaniasis, and West Nile Virus. Each disease has potential long-term effects. For instance, brucellosis is potentially associated with arthritis, deafness, optic neuritis, sensorineural hearing loss, and Guillain-Barre syndrome. Q fever is potentially associated with chronic hepatitis, osetomyelitis, and post Q fever chronic fatigue syndrome. Moreover, West Nile virus can manifest as variable physical, functional, or cognitive disabilities.

Total Disability Rating Based on Individual Unemployability (TDIU or IU)

A veteran will receive compensation at the 100% disability rating level if his/her service connected disabilities prevent the veteran from being able to get a job and keep the job. A Total Disability Rating Based on Individual Unemployability (TDIU or IU) is possible even if the veteran's service connected condition does not equal a 100% disability rating.

Obtaining a 100% schedular rating can be difficult if you are trying to combine multiple disabilities in order to reach a total rating. The alternative IU route can make it easier to gain those same benefits. If you have disabilities related to service which prevent you from being able to hold a job then you should be eligible for IU.

Unemployability is the VA's way of admitting that, in spite of the assigned ratings that do not combine to a 100% rating, some veterans still cannot work due to their disabilities. The VA determines a veteran's entitlement to IU in the context of the individual veteran's capabilities, regardless of whether an average person would be rendered unemployable under the same circumstances.

In this short guide, we will discuss some common questions about IU so you know what the VA is looking for when it decides these claims.

1. How do I know if I'm eligible for IU?

What constitutes eligibility for IU? VA regulations provide that if a veteran cannot work—cannot engage in substantially gainful employment—due to service connected conditions, he or she is unemployable. "Gainful employment" is defined as the ability to hold a job which pays more than or equal to the poverty level set by the federal government.

The primary consideration in determining whether or not a veteran is entitled to IU is whether his or her service connected disabilities prevent him or her from obtaining and maintaining substantially gainful employment. In other words, are you able to find a job that pays enough to put your earnings over the poverty level? And are you capable of keeping such a job if you are able to find one? If your service connected physical or mental disabilities impair your ability to find and keep a job, you may be entitled to IU.

2. What are the scheduler requirements for IU?

When the VA is evaluating a claim for IU, the first thing it will look at is whether the veteran meets the schedular requirements for IU. They are as follows:

• Veterans with only one service connected condition must be rated greater than or equal to 60% for that condition;

• Veterans with two or more service connected conditions must have at least one condition rated greater than or equal to 40% with a combined rating greater than or equal to 70%.

For the purposes of the IU regulation, the following combinations may be considered a "single disability":

• Disabilities of one or both upper extremities, or lower extremities, including the bilateral factor

• Disabilities resulting from a common etiology or single accident

• Disabilities affecting a single body system (i.e., orthopedic, respiratory)

• Multiple injuries incurred in action

• Multiple disabilities incurred as a POW

For example: A veteran suffers from several service connected heart disabilities such as diabetes and diabetic retinopathy and neuropathy. These disabilities arise from a common etiology (the veteran's diabetes mellitus). Therefore, according to regulations, the rating for these disabilities need only combine to a 60% evaluation in order for the veteran to qualify for TDIU under 4.16(a).

Another example, a veteran has been service connected for his Lumbar Spine condition at 40%, his left knee at 30%, and his PTSD condition at 30%. Following the combined ratings math used by the VA, the veteran's total percentage is 70%. Because the veteran has one service connected disability rated at 40%, and because his total rating is 70%, the veteran meets the schedular requirements for IU.

There are a few important things to remember about the schedular requirements for IU. First, when making a determination on IU, the VA can only consider disabilities that have already been service connected. If a veteran is service connected for his knees and his back, but in reality could not work due to his PTSD-related anger outbursts (which have not been service connected but are part of a pending claim), the VA will only consider the knees and the back when deciding if the veteran can work or not. Until service connection is granted for PTSD (if at all), the veteran must prove that he cannot work due to his knees and back condition alone, as opposed to the PTSD.

Second, and on a related note, the VA cannot consider non-service connected disabilities when making a determination on IU. For example, if a veteran has a 70% service connected rating for PTSD and a non-service connected back disability, the VA must review the veteran's ability to work solely as it pertains to the service connected PTSD. Even if the veteran is receiving worker's compensation or Social Security Disability for the back injury, which would indicate that another governmental organization recognized that the veteran could not work due to his back, the VA cannot use this information against the veteran. After all, the veteran may not be able to work for more than one reason.

Also note that the age of the veteran is not a factor when qualifying for IU. This means the VA cannot say that because the veteran is a certain age he or she would not be able to work due to the veteran's age alone.

3. What if I don't meet the scheduler requirements for IU?

If you do not meet the 60%/single disability or 70% combined/40% single disability requirement, it still may be possible for you to be awarded IU. VA regulation 38 C.F.R. § 4.16(b) recognizes that some veterans will be unable to work because of their service connected disabilities, but may not meet the schedular requirements. In such cases, the claim is submitted to the Director of the Compensation and Pension Service for extraschedular consideration. The regional office is required to prepare a "full statement as to the veteran's service connected disabilities, employment history, educational and vocational attainment and all other factors bearing on the issue." As you can imagine, this is not a quick process, and receiving an award of IU based on extraschedular consideration can take a long time. Also, note that it is very rare for the Regional Office to refer a claim for IU for extraschedular consideration without a specific request from the veteran for consideration under 38 C.F.R. § 4.16(b), so if you believe your claim warrants such consideration, it is best to make the request sooner rather than later.

The standard for awarding IU on an extraschedular basis is that the case must present an exceptional or unusual disability picture with factors such as marked interference with employment or frequent periods of hospitalization so to render impractical the application of the regular schedular standards. Because these cases are granted on an individual basis, it is a good idea to present evidence that shows why the veteran's particular circumstances render him or her unable to work, such as work background, education background, and periods of hospitalization. Again, note that these are very difficult cases to win, but not impossible. The best thing you can do is gather as much evidence as possible, including an independent medical opinion, which shows that your unique circumstances render you unable to work due to marked interference with employment or frequent periods of hospitalization.

4. How do I apply for IU?

Interestingly enough, you may have already applied for IU without knowing it. A claim for entitlement to IU is not always a separate, free-standing claim. A veteran can file VA Form 21-8940, Application for Increased Compensation Based on Unemployability, at any time to establish a claim for IU. However, if the issue of unemployability is properly raised by the record in conjunction with a claim for service connection or a claim for increased rating, then the VA should consider the issue as part and parcel of the underlying claim, whether or not the veteran has specifically requested IU. But note, it is very rare for the VA to adjudicate the issue of IU without the veteran raising the claim first, and the VA Regional Office will not grant IU without the veteran submitting VA Form 8940, so if you think you are eligible for IU, it is better to initiate the claim yourself by submitting the required form.

VA Form 8940 is a rather complex and confusing form. Section I of the form deals with Disability and Medical Treatment. In this section, the veteran is asked to answer what disability keeps him or her from working. Remember, the veteran's service connected disabilities must be the primary reason he or she is unable to

work. If there are any non-service connected disabilities involved, then the veteran should get a statement from a doctor as to why the non-service connected disabilities are not a factor in the veteran being unable to work. There is also a place on the form for the veteran to provide the name and address of the physician or hospital that is treating him or her for the service connected disabilities. It is very important to state the frequency (monthly, weekly, every other week, etc.) rather than specific dates for the medical provider to whom the veteran goes for treatment relating to his or her particular disabilities.

Section II of the form asks for all employment history for the five-year period preceding the date on which the veteran claims to have become too disabled to work. So, for example, if a veteran stopped working in 2010, work history from 2005-2010 would need to be provided, along with the names and addresses of the employers, what type of work was performed, how many hours per week, and the dates of employment.

Finally, Section III addresses schooling and other training. In this section the veteran is asked whether he or she acquired any other education or training before becoming too disabled to work, or had any education or training since becoming too disabled to work, and specifically what kind of education or training it was. In this, and every section of the form, accurate and specific information supplied by the veteran goes a long way in helping the VA make a timely decision for IU.

It is important to understand that IU is not a freestanding claim, but is part of the rating process. For example, the VA grants a veteran a 70% rating for PTSD, but does not adjudicate the issue of IU. The veteran may think, "Okay, now I have a 70% rating so I can apply for IU," when it fact what he should do is file a Notice of Disagreement to the decision granting the 70% rating for failure to adjudicate the issue of IU. This is important because of the way the VA determines the effective date for IU.

The effective date for IU is often something that the VA gets wrong. In simplest terms, to determine the effective date for IU you must first figure out the date on which the VA first received evidence from some source which indicates that the veteran was unemployable. This could be a letter from a doctor or a notation in medical records which states that the veteran is unable to work due to his or her service connected disability. Second, you must determine the status of the veteran's claims, if any, at the time the VA received this evidence.

There are three main ways to answer the second question. The first possibility is that the VA first received evidence of the veteran's unemployability when he or she filed a claim for service connection or when the VA was considering whether to grant service connection. If the VA eventually grants service connection for the veteran's disability and awards IU, the effective date for the IU would be the date the VA received the claim for service connection or the date the veteran first became unemployable due to his or her service connected disabilities, whichever is later.

If the VA first received evidence of the veteran's unemployability after the VA granted service connection, but before the VA made a final decision on the rating for the disability, the effective date for an award of IU would be the date the VA received the claim for service connection or the date the veteran first became unemployable due to his or her service connected disabilities, whichever is later.

And finally, if the VA first received evidence of the veteran's unemployability when he or she filed a claim for an increased disability rating or while a claim for an increased disability rating is pending, the effective date for an award of IU would be the date the VA received the claim for an increase in disability rating or the date the veteran first became unemployable due to his or her service connected disability ratings, whichever is later.

5. Am I automatically disqualified from consideration for IU because I have a job?

No. In fact, unemployability does not always mean that a veteran is not working. The key, however, is that all income earned from employment must be at or below the poverty level, or from a job that is considered to be "sheltered". These types of marginal employment are not considered as substantially gainful occupation. Marginal employment is considered as "earned annual income that does not exceed the poverty threshold for one person as established by the US Department of Commerce, Bureau of the Census." For 2014, the poverty level for which a veteran must be working under was $11,670. Alternatively, a job in a "sheltered environment" (such as a family business, sheltered workshop, or a position tailored to the specific needs of the veteran) is considered to be marginal employment, even if that job earns an income over the current poverty threshold.

Sheltered employment means that you are given concessions due to your service connected disabilities that would not normally be given to other employees. For example: A veteran with PTSD works for a family friend's business. The family friend provides the veteran with an office and duties that afford limited interaction with other people. The veteran's salary pays his bills, and is over the current poverty threshold. Because the veteran's job has been tailored to his individual needs (limited interaction with other people), his job is considered to be sheltered, and therefore falls under "marginal employment." The VA cannot consider this job as being substantially gainful employment, and must not use it against him in determining IU.

One thing that the VA often overlooks is the requirement that a veteran be able to maintain substantially gainful employment. For instance, a veteran may be able to hold a job for a few months, but then loses the job due to his service connected disabilities. He then may be able to get another job for a few months, before losing that one, and the cycle repeats. In such a case, the veteran is able to get jobs, but he is not maintaining employment, and is eligible for IU.

So, what does this mean on a practical level? First, it means that VA law does allow for some veterans who work to also receive IU benefits at the same time, depending on the circumstances. Second, it means that disabled veterans who are working should not automatically assume that they are not eligible for IU simply because they work.

6. What evidence do I need to support my claim for IU?

To establish entitlement for IU benefits, both evidence of unemployment due to a service connected condition and support documentation from a medical professional must be obtained. Evidence which may assist you in proving your case could be letters from former co-workers or employers, medical evidence, or evidence from a vocational expert.

The VA also has to consider a veteran's educational and work history when determining if the veteran is entitled to IU. The VA must look at the veteran's prior education and training, and how his current disabilities prevent him from working in the field in which he has been trained. If the veteran has participated in a VA vocational rehabilitation program, and still cannot work due to the service connected disabilities, the VA must also consider this as positive evidence that the veteran cannot maintain substantially gainful employment.

It is also important for earnings to be examined in order to assess if the veteran is above or below the poverty threshold. A veteran can produce substantive proof of earnings through pay stubs, tax returns, employer letters, or a Social Security Earnings Record. If the earnings are above the poverty threshold, an evaluation needs to take place to determine if the veteran is working in a "sheltered" environment as discussed above. The veteran will need corroborating evidence to prove that the workplace is sheltered, for example, an employer letter verifying the excessive accommodations.

When it comes to proving to the VA that a veteran is eligible for IU, the best evidence is a professional opinion from a vocational expert or competent medical doctor concerning the veteran's ability to secure or follow a substantially gainful occupation. The opinion should say it is more likely than not that you are unable to work due to your service connected disabilities. Again, the key here is "service connected."

The VA often will schedule a veteran for a Compensation & Pension (C&P) exam to get an opinion on IU. The exam report must include a rationale as to whether it is as likely as not that the service connected disability or combined disabilities render the veteran unable to secure and maintain substantially gainful employment. Additionally, the exam report must also include and describe the functional impairment caused by the veteran's disabilities and how that impairment impacts physical and sedentary employment.

One thing to keep in mind is that if a veteran has multiple service connected disabilities that contribute to unemployability, the VA will likely send the veteran to separate exams for each condition. Each exam will discuss the veteran's single disability and the functional impairment that the veteran has due to that single disability. For example, a back examiner may say, "The veteran can't stand at all or can't walk, but he could do sedentary work," A migraine examiner may say, "He has to lie down at least once a week for several hours. As long as an employer will give that benefit, then he could work." And then a PTSD examiner may say, "Well, he doesn't get along with people too well, so as long as he's working by himself off somewhere, he's fine."

The problem is that the VA will usually look at these three opinions separately, rather than look at them together in order to create a complete picture of the veteran's disabilities. If that is the case, the best thing to do is get an independent medical opinion that either looks at all the service connected disabilities together, or shows that one service connected disability in particular is the one that renders the veteran unable to work.

One option for an independent medical opinion is a vocational expert, but getting a vocational expert for your case might not be easy for many veterans. If so, another option is going to a VA vocational rehabilitation center and asking for an assessment. Again, it is important that any medical opinion you are able to get regarding your inability to work be limited to only your service connected disabilities.

7. Is my IU rating permanent?

IU is not always permanent, and you may have to undergo periodic medical exams to substantiate the continuation of the award, once granted. But, there are safeguards in place that make it more difficult for the VA to take away an award of IU.

If the VA does not follow its own rules and regulations when proposing a reduction, the reduction is considered void and unlawful. If the VA has determined that your current disability rating warrants reduction, it must first issue a notice of proposed reduction. This first notice gives you sixty days to submit evidence to show that your condition has not improved. You also have an option to request a pre-determination hearing within thirty days of the notice. Requesting a hearing may buy you additional time to submit evidence.

> **The VA has the burden to demonstrate that actual employability has been established by clear and convincing evidence in order to reduce or sever IU. This is a very high burden to meet.**

Furthermore, there are several protections set forth in the regulations against a proposed reduction. One of those protections is for 100% ratings when based on unemployability (IU or IU). The VA has the burden to demonstrate that actual employability has been established by clear and convincing evidence in order to reduce or sever IU. This is a very high burden to meet. Even if you are working, you are allowed to keep your IU for a full year. However, in cases where the veteran has not returned to work, then the VA has to have really good evidence to discontinue IU.

Under the regulations, if the VA determines that the veteran has sustained improvement and that such improvement warrants reduction of an IU rating, but the record reflects that the veteran is unable to engage in substantial gainful employment, then IU must be preserved. In other words, in cases where your disability has materially improved, your IU rating can still be protected from reduction if the evidence continues to show that you are unable to work due to your service connected disability.

If you submit evidence prior to the expiration of the first sixty day notice, there is a possibility that the VA will find reasonable basis to send you for a re-examination. If it decides to do so, the final rating action is deferred pending the outcome of the new examination. A very important point is that an examination that is the basis for reduction must be as thorough as the examination that established the current rating. Attending the examination is very important. If you do not show up, your benefits can be automatically reduced or terminated. If you are unable to attend on the date scheduled, you must call and reschedule, or have a very good reason explaining your absence.

The VA must review all of the new evidence, including the report of re-examination, in the context of the entire record. The VA will then issue a final rating decision. The second rating decision starts a new sixty day period. The implementation of the reduction goes into effect on the last day of the month of the second decision.

This means that even if the VA reduces a disability rating, it can't take away IU unless it has evidence of marked improvement that is clear and convincing, unequivocally demonstrating that you have regained the physical or mental capacity to return to the workforce on a sustained basis.

Posttraumatic Stress Disorder (PTSD)

Posttraumatic Stress Disorder (PTSD) is a mental illness that can occur after a traumatic event such as combat, physical abuse, sexual assault, terrorist attack, serious accident or a natural disaster. Even though diagnosis of PTSD did not come about until 1980, as long as there has been war there has been soldiers suffering this illness. It was just given different names such as "shell shock," "soldier's heart," "combat exhaustion," or "Stress Response Syndrome." But PTSD doesn't affect just service members who see combat. Anyone who is exposed to a life threatening event can develop PTSD.

Veterans have had difficulty getting the VA to acknowledge the effects PTSD has had on them. Even though PTSD can devastate a person's ability to maintain relationships with loved ones and to hold a job the VA does not do a great job recognizing a veteran's PTSD being related to service and properly rating it.

PTSD is the only mental illness to have its own VA regulation. To be service connected for PTSD, the VA requires (1) a diagnosis of PTSD; (2) a link, established by medical evidence, between current symptoms and an in-service stressor; and (0) credible supporting evidence that the claimed in-service stressor occurred

In order for the VA to recognize a veteran's PTSD in a service connected compensation claim, the diagnosis of PTSD must be provided by a qualified medical professional. Even though many veterans are treated by the VA or private therapists who are not doctors or psychologists (i.e. licensed mental health social

workers, licensed counselors, etc.), the VA will not accept their opinions initially diagnosing PTSD.

In addition, the diagnosis must conform to the diagnostic criteria in the DSM-V. The most common reason the VA denies a claim for PTSD is because it determines that a veteran does not meet all of the diagnostic criteria in the DSM-V for PTSD. A veteran may be suffering from extreme PTSD, but if his or her symptoms do not fall neatly within the diagnostic criteria for PTSD, then, for VA purposes, the veteran does not have PTSD, and service connection will be denied. The diagnostic criteria in the DSM-V for PTSD may be found on the VA website.

The VA eases the second requirement of credible supporting evidence in a few circumstances. In the situations outlined below, the veteran's lay testimony alone—without credible evidence of the in-service stressor—may establish the occurrence of the in-service stressor. These situations include:

(1) If the evidence establishes a diagnosis of PTSD during service and the claimed stressor is related to that service.

(2) If a veteran's claimed stressor is related to the veteran's fear of hostile military or terrorist activity, such as exposure to explosive devices, small arms fire, or suspected sniper attacks, and a VA psychiatrist or psychologist confirms both that the stressor is adequate to support a diagnosis of PTSD and that the veteran's symptoms are related to the claimed stressor.

(3) If the evidence establishes that the veteran is a prisoner-of-

war and the claimed stressor is related to that POW experience.

(4) If the evidence establishes that the veteran engaged in combat with the enemy and the stressor is related to that combat.

Additionally, for veterans who suffered an in-service personal or sexual assault (military sexual trauma or MST), the veteran does not need an official record of the stressor. The VA will consider records other than the veteran's service records to be "credible supporting evidence" of the stressor. These records include, but are not limited to, records from law enforcement authorities, rape crisis centers, mental health counseling centers, hospitals, or physicians; and statements from family members, roommates, fellow service members, or clergy.

Moreover, evidence of behavioral changes following the claimed assault will be considered, too. Examples of behavior changes include a request for a transfer to another military duty assignment, deterioration in work performance, substance abuse, and episodes of depression. The veteran can also show changes in behavior by having family and friends speak to the changes in the veteran from before service to after service. Importantly, again, the veteran does not need an official record of the assault.

If a veteran's claim for PTSD does not fit into one of the above categories, there must be evidence that corroborates the occurrence of the stressor, meaning credible supporting evidence that the claimed in-service stressor occurred. The supporting evidence must include more than the veteran's own testimony. Unless there is no reasonable possibility that assistance by the VA is required to aid in proving the claim, the VA must assist the veteran in developing evidence that supports the existence of a stressor.

For the veteran's service records to corroborate the stressor, they do not need to include every detail of the event. If there is independent evidence showing a stressful event occurred and that evidence shows the veteran's personal exposure to the event, this could be sufficient corroborative evidence. In addition, credible supporting evidence can come from lay sources such as buddy statements.

The final step of establishing service connection for PTSD is proving a causal nexus between the current symptomatology and the claimed in-service stressor. This step requires an opinion by a medical expert. The evidence must show that the stressor was at least a contributory cause of the current symptoms. As long as there is a relationship between the stressor encountered in service and the current diagnosis of PTSD, a veteran whose service medical records show no evidence of a mental disorder can be entitled to service connection for PTSD, even if the PTSD develops many years after service.

For a medical nexus opinion to be adequate, the doctor must review the relevant records about the veteran's stressor. These most likely would include service medical records, service treatment records, current treatment records and any C&P exams. A medical opinion that relies just on a veteran's statement to the doctor will fail due to the doctor not reviewing all the other evidence in the case. The best place to find all the relevant evidence is in the veteran's Claims File, also known as the C file. This file contains all the evidence from every claim the veteran has filed since service. It should also contain the veteran's service medical records and service records.

The VA's Definition of Alcohol Abuse and Drug Abuse

The VA defines willful misconduct related to alcohol as drinking to enjoy intoxicating effects. In the same way, the VA defines willful misconduct related to drugs as the progressive and frequent use of drugs to the point of addiction.

> **Direct service connection may be granted only when a disability is not the result of the veteran's willful misconduct or the result of alcohol or drug abuse. Yet, simply drinking alcoholic beverages or infrequently using drugs in isolation is not considered abuse or willful misconduct.**

When making a determination on whether a disability that involves alcohol or drug abuse will be service connected, there are three categories of disabilities:

(1) Disabilities from voluntary and willful alcohol or drug abuse that develop during service. Service connection is not awarded for these types of alcohol/drug abuse disabilities.

(2) Disabilities caused by alcohol or drug abuse that are secondary to a service connected condition. In these cases, service connection may be awarded for the resulting disability.

For example, consider a veteran who is service connected for PTSD and develops alcoholism secondary to his PTSD. If the veteran later develops cirrhosis of the liver due to alcoholism, the veteran would be entitled to service connection for the cirrhosis.

(3) Disabilities aggravated by alcohol or drug abuse that are secondary to a service connected condition. Here, service connection may be awarded for these disabilities. For instance, consider a veteran who is service connected for PTSD, suffers from alcoholism due to the PTSD, and also has Diabetes Mellitus II. If the veteran's alcoholism aggravates his Diabetes Mellitus II, then the veteran would be entitled to service connected compensation for his Diabetes Mellitus II.

In the same way, the VA will not grant compensation benefits for a disability that was caused by the veteran's use of tobacco products during the veteran's service. However, it may grant compensation benefits for a disability caused by the veteran's use of tobacco if that use was caused by a service connected disability.

How & Where Do I File a Claim?

A claim for service connected compensation may be filed several different ways:

1. Online through the Veterans On-line Application
http://vabenefits.vba.va.gov/vonapp/main.asp

2. Online through the E-benefits portal
https://www.ebenefits.va.gov/ebenefits-portal/ebenefits.portal

3. Via mail. To download a paper copy of the application, go to
http://www.vba.va.gov/pubs/forms/VBA-21-526EZ-ARE.pdf

Claims should be filed with the VA Regional Office in the state where the veteran resides. There are 58 ROs across the country. Every state in the United States has at least one Regional Office.

There are also Regional Offices in Puerto Rico and the Philippines, as well as in Washington, D.C.

The addresses for these offices can be found by accessing this link http://benefits.va.gov/benefits/offices.asp.

There is no time limit to file a claim for disability benefits. However, as a general rule, the effective date of an award will almost always be the date the Regional Office receives the claim. The effective date controls the amount of retroactive benefits a veteran can receive and is discussed later in greater detail. An exception to this general rule is when a veteran applies within one year of discharge. Here, entitlement can be established retroactively to the separation date.

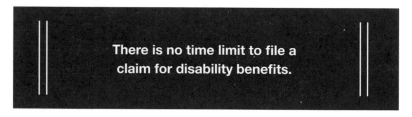

There is no time limit to file a claim for disability benefits.

A veteran can start a claim by simply filing a note that indicates an intent to apply for benefits and identifies the benefits sought. This is called an informal claim. Nonetheless, in order to preserve the claim's effective date as the date the veteran filed the informal claim, a veteran must file a formal application (VA Form 21-526) within the year that the Regional Office received the informal claim.

Any correspondence submitted to the VA (claim forms, evidence, etc.) should include your claim number. Similarly, it is a good idea to send all documents via certified mail return receipt requested.

The VCAA Notice Letter

After the Regional Office (RO) receives a complete or substantially complete application, it must notify you of any information and evidence necessary to substantiate the claim. This letter is referred to as a "development letter" or a "VCAA notice letter" (Veterans' Claims Assistance Act), mandated by the VA's "duty to notify" and "duty to assist." This letter will identify the information and evidence that you should provide, as well as the evidence that the RO will attempt to obtain. The letter will request that you provide any evidence in your possession that pertains to the claim.

If you fail to respond to the RO's request for evidence, the RO may decide the claim based on the existing evidence in the file. However, if the RO issues a decision, and you subsequently provide additional evidence within one year of the date of the notice letter, the RO must decide the claim again and consider the new evidence.

Compensation and Pension Examinations

The VA's duty to assist also includes providing a medical examination or obtaining a medical opinion when such an examination or opinion is necessary to make a decision on the claim. A medical examination or opinion is considered necessary if the evidence of record contains competent evidence that the veteran has a current disability and indicates that the disability may be associated with the veteran's service.

The Compensation and Pension (C&P) examination department is part of the Veterans Health Administration. The VA also contracts with outside providers to perform these examinations. A veteran who is scheduled for a C&P examination must appear at that examination. When a veteran fails, without good cause, to report for a C&P examination, the VA must decide the claim based on the evidence of record, and can deny the claim. Please note that this exam is practically never performed by the veteran's treating doctor, even if the exam is conducted at the same facility.

Here are some important things for a veteran to consider about the exam:

• Arrive on time. Expect to wait but being on time is important.

• Be polite. Give the examiner the benefit of the doubt that he is there to help you.

• Be honest and forthright. When the examiner asks you how you are, this is the time your exam really starts. Tell the examiner exactly how you are. This is not a polite question that you would ask someone when first meeting them. This is the first question of the exam. Most veterans are conditioned to not complain. If you have trouble stating how you are, it's safe to say, "I've had better days." After all, if you were "okay", you wouldn't be at a C&P exam.

• Bring a written list of symptoms, even embarrassing symptoms, to help refresh your memory during the exam. What veterans sometimes feel are unimportant details could very well be the key to success in the claim.

• Take a witness to the examination. It can be a spouse, adult child, or close friend. A witness is important because it is very easy for veterans to forget important details about the exam, let alone deal with the normal stress that veterans experience when being evaluated by the VA's C&P examiners. If possible, the veteran should take the witness into the exam room with them; however, this request is frequently denied by the VA. If the request to take a witness into the examination is denied, it is important that the veteran proceed with the exam. Failure to cooperate with a C&P examination can result in denial of the claim.

• If one of the veteran's treating medical providers has provided a favorable opinion in the matter, it does not hurt for the veteran to give the favorable opinion to the C&P examiner for consideration.

• Do not complain about the VA system in general. A C&P exam is not the time to air grievances. (For example, how long you waited, how long you've had this claim in, what the nurse said to you when you called…)

• Ask for the examiner's business card, so that the veteran can ensure that the person doing the examination was actually the one who wrote and signed the final report.

The Rating Decision

Once all the evidence has been developed and received by the Regional Office, it will issue a Rating Decision (RD). The RD lets the veteran know which claims have been granted or denied. If the VA grants service connection, then the rating decision will focus on the following:

The Rating

Your disability rating depends on the severity of your condition. It is based on the criteria laid out in the VA's rating schedule, a list that encompasses hundreds of different medical conditions. The VA assigns disability evaluations from 0% to 100% in 10% increments. A 100% disability rating is also called a total rating because it means that a veteran is totally disabled.

Regardless of the rating, the important thing is to have the VA grant service connection, even if it initially rates your disability or disabilities at 0%. With an award of service connection, even with a 0% rating, you have a right to seek an increased rating if the condition gets worse. Plus, when you are in receipt of two or more separate non-compensable permanent service connected disabilities of such a character that clearly interfere with normal employability, the VA is authorized to assign a 10% disability rating.

The disability rating determines the compensation amount. The higher the disability evaluation, the higher the monthly compensation payment. The dollar amount of the payment at each rating level is exactly the same for everyone, whether a veteran makes a million dollars, or no money at all. The difference between a 10% compensation rating and a 100% rating is significant. As of December 2014, a 10% rating is worth $133.17 per month; a 100% rating is worth $2,906.83. With a spouse or other dependents, the monthly amount increases.

The Effective Date

In addition to the disability rating, the Rating Decision will include the effective date assigned for the award of benefits. The effective

|| **The effective date is usually the date the veteran files the claim.** ||

date is usually the date the veteran filed the claim. As mentioned earlier, the effective date controls the amount of retroactive benefits to which a veteran is entitled.

There are a few exceptions to the general rule regarding the assignment of an effective date.

First, if a claim is filed within one year of separation from service, then the effective date for benefits would be the latter of (1) the day after the date of separation or (2) the post-service date the disability is documented by medical records.

Moreover, for claims for an increased rating of an already service connected condition, the effective date will be the date the disability is shown to have increased in severity, with the potential to go as far back as one year prior to the filing date.

Finally, if the VA denies a claim for disability compensation and later obtains service records not previously associated with the veteran's file that are relied on to grant benefits, then the effective date could be as early as the date the original claim was filed.

Notice of Disagreement (NOD)

If a veteran does not agree with the RO's decision, that decision may be appealed to the Board of Veterans' Appeals. To initiate this appeal process requires filing a Notice of Disagreement (NOD).

There are several reasons for filing a Notice of Disagreement to a Rating Decision. The VA may have failed to service connect your disability; it may have granted a low rating for your condition; or it may have awarded an incorrect effective date.

Before 2015 an NOD was filed by filling out a Statement in Support of Claim (VA Form 21-4138) or by a letter that simply expressed disagreement with the denial of benefits and an intent to appeal the decision. However, VA now mandates that a veteran file an NOD by using its VA Form 21-0958. Make sure you mail the NOD via return receipt certified mail within one year from the date of the notice of action (please note that the VA has been trying to reduce the appeal period to less than one year. Make sure to check the VA decision to verify the appeal period length), because the date the Regional Office receives the NOD is critical in continuing your appeal rights.

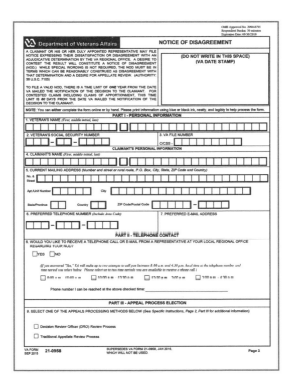

NOD Acknowledgment and Appeal Selection

Once the RO processes the NOD, the RO will send an appeal selection letter, asking, the veteran to choose a method for the review of the Rating Decision. A veteran may choose between the traditional review process or a review by a decision review officer.

In a traditional review, someone new is reviewing the file and RD. Unless new evidence is submitted, the RO will likely not make any changes to the previous RD.

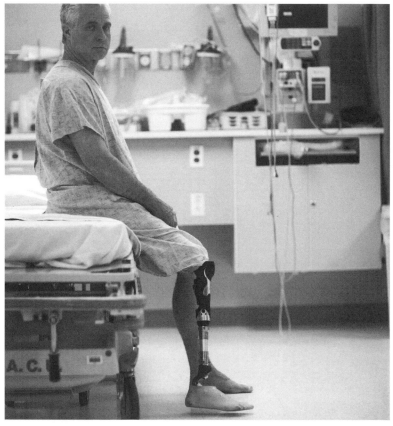

In contrast, a review by a decision review officer provides a new review by a senior level adjudicator. The decision review officer will review the claim without deference to the prior RD. This method allows the veteran to obtain a hearing with the decision review officer, or an informal telephone conference.

If the RO decides to grant the claim or alter the prior decision in any way, the RO will issue a new RD. If the RO upholds its prior decision, it will issue a Statement of the Case (SOC).

Substantive Appeal

The Substantive Appeal is the final document required to perfect the appeal. Think of it this way: a NOD initiates an appeal, and the substantive appeal (VA Form 9) completes it.

The appeal to the BVA may be filed on a VA Form 9 or in another writing that contains all of the information requested in the VA Form 9.

The deadline to submit the VA Form 9 is the later of either.

- One year from the Rating Decision notice letter, or
- Sixty days from the date of the SOC notice letter no matter how much time has elapsed since the Rating Decision.

RO Certification of Appeal and BVA Docketing Notice

After you file a Substantive Appeal to the RO, the RO will certify your appeal to the Board of Veterans' Appeals. It can take years for the RO to certify your case to the BVA. The VA has never adequately explained this delay, but following a substantive appeal, the case does not go immediately to the BVA.

When the RO certifies your appeal to the BVA, you will be notified in the form of a letter which is commonly called the "90 day letter." This letter explains that you have up to ninety days to request a change in representation, request a personal hearing, and/or submit additional evidence. Beware: the BVA can make its decision prior to the expiration of ninety days. Once your file has been received by the BVA, the BVA will send a notice that your appeal has been docketed.

Hearings

At the BVA, you have several options regarding a hearing: (1) no BVA hearing at all; (2) an in-person BVA hearing in Washington, D.C.; (3) an in-person BVA hearing with a travel Board member at your local RO office; or (4) a video conference hearing at your local RO with a Board member in D.C.

The Decision by the Board of Veterans' Appeals

The Board will issue a written decision on the appeal. It may (1) grant, (2) deny, (3) remand, (4) refer, or (5) dismiss the appeal for each of the claims. The decision by the BVA is a final decision for all issues addressed in the "Order" section of the decision. If the Board chooses to remand an issue to the local RO for additional development, then a "Remand" section follows the "Order." A remanded issue cannot be appealed to the Court of Appeals for Veterans' Claims because a remand is not a final, appealable decision. A referral is when the BVA believes that the Regional Office did not make a decision on the issue yet and the Regional Office must make the first decision for the BVA to then review it.

Appealing a Decision made by the Board of Veterans' Appeals

To appeal a decision by the BVA, you may file an appeal to the United States Court of Appeals for Veterans' Claims (Court or CAVC). It is important to know that you have only 120 days from the date of the BVA decision to file a Notice of Appeal to the Court. Alternatively, rather than appealing the Board's decision, you may choose to reopen your claim at the local Regional Office by submitting new and material evidence. Choosing this option, however, does not protect the effective date of your original claim, and you will probably lose retroactive benefits that could have been preserved by filing an appeal.

Awards

If the CAVC or the BVA grants the claim, the file goes back to the RO to implement the decision.

The RO will issue a new rating decision. If the CAVC or BVA grants only the issue of service connection, and does not address the rating or effective date, the RO will need to decide those issues.

Appeals Reform

The VA has been lobbying Congress for some time now to change the structure of the appeals process. At this moment, the laws governing the VA appeals process have not been changed but there has been strong support for this change in both Houses of Congress and the White House. Even though there is no final law as of yet, the VA has laid out its plan in proposed legislation.

The essence of the change is to strongly encourage veterans to stop filing appeals. The VA is hoping to stop appeals by severely limiting the evidence that a veteran can file after a rating decision while letting the veteran refile a claim and keep the effective date of the original claim. The VA will still allow appeals to the BVA. It will cut out the middle step of an SOC that is issued by the Regional Office so that once a NOD is filed then the case goes directly to the BVA. There are three different types of appeals to the BVA. The first type is a closed record where the veteran does not ask for a hearing and does not request to let any new evidence in the record. This is the fastest lane. The second lane involves cases where the veteran wants to add evidence. The third is where the veteran wants a hearing and to put in more evidence. The VA says that by reducing the time the veteran is allowed to put in new evidence in his C file it will reduce the time it takes the VA to make a decision. The VA is requesting that the law not make the VA decide the case in a specific amount of time.

As of the printing of this book none of these changes have become law yet. But it is important to research these changes before filing a claim to understand your options. You will be able to find out more information about this topic at www.hillandponton.com/veterans-law-blog/.

Hiring an Attorney

When you do NOT need an attorney for your VA claim

The VA service connected disability process can be very confusing and complicated but it can also be straightforward. There are many claims—in fact, the majority of claims—for which you do not need a paid attorney to help you with them. Do not hire an attorney in these situations.

1. Any first time claim. This includes an original claim, a claim for increase, or a reopened claim. In these situations, VA has a duty under the law to help you win your claim by getting any service records, Social Security records, VA medical records and private medical records that you tell VA are important to your claim. VA must also send you to one of their doctors, a C&P exam, if there is need for a medical opinion to win your case. In these situations you need to submit evidence or let the VA know where to get it, but you should make the VA fulfill its duty.

2. An appeal for dependent benefits. The VA often fails to pay a veteran for dependent benefits when a veteran wins service connected benefits. A veteran could hire an attorney here to appeal it but it would be easier and much faster to apply online through Ebenefits. A veteran service officer (VSO) can handle this claim for a veteran as well.

3. Denial of benefits on a Rating Decision due to missing a C&P exam. There has been a lot of information in the news of late where the VA 'sets' C&P exams for which the veteran never

received notice. Then the VA turned around and denied benefits on this basis. Additionally, there are times where a veteran does not get notice of the C&P exam because it goes to the wrong address or the veteran has a conflict. In these situations, it would be best to not appeal but to write a letter to the VA and explain why the veteran was unable to attend the C&P exam. Remember, the veteran has a year to appeal the decision. Writing a letter about why the veteran could not attend and then asking for a new exam is potentially a faster way to get the proper benefits. Now, if there is no response to the letter asking for a new exam after several months then the veteran should consider appealing. The appeal will take longer—most likely years—but if the VA is not going to respond to the request for a new exam it is better to move the case forward.

4. When you are confident in what you need to prove the claim. Was the VA missing evidence that you have, and that you know will prove your claim? Can you get a statement from your doctor to prove it? If you are confident that you have the evidence you need then you do not need an advocate.

The decision to hire an attorney to represent you for your VA disability compensation claim is an extremely important one. If you are going to pay an advocate then that advocate must be able to do more for your claim than the free representation that you can get from a VSO. Once you sign a contract with an attorney you cannot get out of it. So here are three things to consider before signing a contract:

1. Does the attorney have something more to show than just VA

accreditation? Any attorney who holds himself out as a veteran's attorney has to be "accredited" by the VA. Please understand to gain "accreditation" means that the attorney only had to watch a three hour video. The VA has thousands of regulations and rules. Three hours is not enough to even do an overview of these. Further, most VSOs have more rigorous training than this; VSOs do not charge for representation. If the attorney holds out being "accredited" as the only experience that he has in VA law that is a red flag. If this is all the experience and training the attorney has, that means that the attorney will be using your case to get training. His errors could undermine your case. Obtaining your benefits are too important for someone else's training. You want an attorney that has practiced in this area for at least several years. You want to see a resume that shows expertise in the field. You want to see someone who is involved in the advocate community, teaching others and writing papers or books on how to represent veterans.

2. Does the attorney focus on VA claims? You want to see an attorney that is focused on VA benefits. This area of law is complicated and requires constant training and studying of the law as it changes. If you see a firm practicing many areas of law, this is a red flag, and you want to look and see if there are attorneys in the firm that only practice VA law. If not, you are trusting your case to someone who doesn't specialize in this area.

3. Insist on speaking with an attorney before signing a contract. Your VA claim is important to you. It is personal. Hiring an attorney is a big decision. You need to speak with the attorney before signing the contract. You need to see what they can do to help you

with your claim. An attorney should have time before you sign to tell you how he can help you with your claim. Remember, you are agreeing to pay this attorney; make sure that you are going to get your money's worth. Importantly, once you sign a contract with an attorney, that contract is irrevocable. If you fire that attorney, he or she can still demand a portion of your retroactive benefits. This right would prevent any other attorney from representing you. Bottom line: if the attorney doesn't have time to speak with you before you agree to hire him, do not hire him.

Conclusion

Although the journey to service connected benefits is often long and confusing, we hope this book has given you the knowledge you need to face the hurdles ahead. If you feel you are entitled to service connected benefits, do not give up.

Obtaining the service connected compensation and the correct rating is a difficult process. But it is important to remember that you represented our country, which means that you are entitled to the rights of being compensated for your service connected disabilities. If the VA keeps denying your claim and you need help please give us a call. We represent veterans all across the nation. We know where the VA falls short in their decisions and how to overcome the VA's shortcomings and win benefits for our clients.

We would be more than happy to review your claim, without charge. Additionally, we have a 90-day satisfaction guarantee. If you are unsatisfied with our representation then you can walk away and we will tear up your contract and waive any fee.

For additional and current information, please visit our website and blog at hillandponton.com.

COMMON VA ABBREVIATIONS AND ACRONYMS

AO   Agent Orange

AOJ   Agency of Original Jurisdiction
Usually just means RO (Regional Office).

AMC   Appeals Management Center
Where BVA sometimes sends a case for further development if it doesn't send it back to the RO.

BVA   Board of Veterans Appeals Or "Board" Located in Washington, D.C. If an appeal is filed to a Rating Decision, claim moves to the BVA.

C-file   Claims file
The file that the VA benefits section keeps on veteran's claims. This file is different from the file that the VA health section keeps on the veteran.

C&P   Compensation & Pension
C&P Service is a part of the VA division that administers benefits. "C&P" most often refers to VA medical exams to determine SC or lack thereof.

CAVC   U.S. Court of Appeals for Veterans' Claims
Or "Veterans' Court" or just "Court"

CUE*   Clear & Unmistakable Error
CUE is not really a "claim," but rather a collateral attack on a final decision. It's actually a request for revision based on CUE. It's the only way you can get EED back to original date of unappealed, final claim but it is extremely difficult to prove the necessary elements.

DBQs   Disability Benefits Questionnaire
This is a form that a veteran can take to his VA or private doctor to describe the extent of the veteran's disability. The VA is supposed to accept this form in lieu of a C&P exam but that is not always the case.

DC   Diagnostic Code
4-digit numbers assigned to various conditions listed in rating schedule. This code is used to rate the veteran's disability.

De Novo Latin for "Do Over"
The adjudicator should not give any weight to the prior decision.

DIC   Dependency & Indemnity Compensation
Widow's (or other survivors') benefit.

DRO   Decision Review Officer
A supervisor at the RO. After you get a RD (rating decision) you want to appeal, you can ask for DRO review first before going on up to BVA.

DTA   Duty to Assist
Addressed by VCAA, described by the VA as "not a one way street," the veteran must also assist the VA with his claim, failure of DTA can be grounds for appeal, but cannot form the basis of CUE.

DVA   Department of Veterans' Affairs
An alternative abbreviation.

ED   Effective Date
With some important exceptions, it is usually the date VA receives the claim, including requests to reopen.

EED   Earlier Effective Date
Facts and circumstances may allow argument for an EED. One way to get it is proving CUE.

EPTS or EPTE   Existed Prior to Service/Entrance
Conditions often noted on entrance exam. The VA can try to deny SC based on EPTS, but if veteran shows a worsening in service, then condition is usually presumed aggravated by service (and therefore SC) and the VA must rebut.

GAF   Global Assessment of Functioning
Common psych test with scores ranging from 0 to 100. The lower the score, the less able a person is to function in work and daily life. GAF has been phased out in the DSM-V.

GWI/GWS Gulf War Illness/Syndrome
"Diagnosed medically unexplained chronic multisymptom illness" or "undiagnosed" illnesses with symptoms similar to fibromyalgia, chronic fatigue, etc.

GWOT   Global War on Terror
An umbrella term for the conflicts beginning after 9/11.

I/R   Increased Rating
Type of claim filed to get higher rating for already SC condition. Veteran just needs to say he thinks problem has worsened. Then he should get a new C&P exam.

IME   Independent Medical Expert/Exam
The BVA sometimes will send a case out for an independent opinion. This is also something that a veteran can obtain to substantiate his/her claim.

IRIS   Inquiry Routing & Information System
On the VA website. A means of contacting them with questions.

JSRRC   Joint Services Records Research Center
Formerly known as USASCRUR or CRUR — Best known as where the VA is supposed to get PTSD stressor confirmation.

M1 - VA Health Care Adjudication Manual
Internal "How-To" book for conducting medical
exams, etc.

M21-1MR VA Claims Adjudication Manual Rewrite
Usually just called M21. The "How-To" book for
managing and evaluating claims. Its provisions are
substantive and have the same authority as VA
regulations.

MPFs/MPRs Military Personnel File/Records
If they could be pertinent to the case, be sure you get
these from NPRC or be sure they are in the C-file.

NARA National Archives & Records Administration
Helpful research source. NPRC is a division of it.

NME or N&M New & Material Evidence
Necessary for reopening. It's easy to get new
evidence. (But it's usually just cumulative). What's
harder to get is evidence that is material and capable
of substantiating the claim. Usually need a good nexus
or quasi-nexus opinion or some strong lay statements
to cross the low materiality threshold.

NOD Notice of Disagreement
What you need to file to appeal a RD. Must be filed
with RO within one year of notice of decision. Tell
which findings you disagree with and why, say you

desire appellate review. NOD may also consist of any pro se correspondence to the VA expressing dissatisfaction with decision.

NPRC   National Personnel Records Center
In St. Louis, where most military records are kept. Site of the legendary 1973 fire that destroyed a lot of records (over 2/3 for those discharged from Army before 1960 and about 2/3 of those discharged from AF before 1964 — certain alphabetical sections. Some records can be reconstructed.

NSC   Non-Service connected
Disabilities often noted on RDs as having been determined (either officially or unofficially) as not related to service. Sometimes a basis for pension as opposed to disability compensation.

OMPF   Official Military Personnel File
Should be available via NPRC.

POW   Prisoner of War
POWs are afforded a broad range of advantages in the disability compensation process, such as having disabilities presumed SC no matter when they manifest themselves.

PTSD   Posttraumatic Stress Disorder
A common mental ailment resulting from service.

QTC   "Quality, Timeliness & Customer Service"
The VA contracts with this company to provide
C&P exams.

R&B   Reasons & Bases
The VA is supposed to provide adequate explanations
for its decisions.

RD   Rating Decision
Explains issues, discusses the applicable law &
evidence relied on, and provides explanation for the
decision. If a rating is not involved, can be titled
"Administrative Decision."

RO   Regional Office
Where most benefits claims originate. Usually the one
nearest to veteran's residence and where the C-file
is kept. Also called VARO. Where you return if BVA
gives you remand.

SC   Service Connected, Service Connection
The first and most important goal in the veteran's
claim.

SMC   Special Monthly Compensation
Extra payment for certain SC conditions, often for
"loss of use" of certain body parts – including
buttocks, feet, hands, etc.

SMRs/STRs Service Medical/Treatment Records
Often essential for establishing SC.

SOC   Statement of the Case
Submitted by the RO after you file an NOD. This is
what you need in order to proceed with a substantive
appeal to the BVA. Usually just an expanded form of
the RD.

SSC or SiSC Statement in Support of Claim (Form 4138)
This is the form to use instead of sworn affidavits for
statements of the veteran, family or friends. Usually
just called 4138s.

SSOC   Supplemental Statement of the Case Comes out after
an SOC, remand, or prior SSOC. Addresses later
issues, clarifies findings, or explains their denial again.

TBI   Traumatic Brain Injury
Unfortunately, the common condition for Iraq/
Afghanistan (OIF/OEF/GWOT) veterans.

TDIU   Total Disability & Individual Unemployability
Also called IU. When a veteran has one SC disability at
least 60% OR if more than one with one at 40% and
combined rating at least 70% - and if a veteran can't
sustain substantially gainful employment, then the
veteran is entitled to 100% rating.

VA   Department of Veterans' Affairs
Also seen as DVA, previously (until 1989) stood for
Veterans "Administration," often used interchangeably
with "Secretary" as in Secretary of Department of VA.

VACO   Veterans Affairs Central Office
Directs VAROs and medical facilities, provides
procedures they're required to follow.

VAMC   VA Medical Center
Usually where C&P exams take place.

VARO   VA Regional Office
Same as RO.

VAE   VA Exam
Just another way of saying C&P exam. The exam to
determine service connection and proper rating.

VBA   Veterans Benefits Administration
In charge of all veterans benefits programs.

VLJ (ALJ)   Veterans Law Judge/Administrative Law Judge
They make the BVA decisions.

VSO   Veterans Service Organization (or Officer)
Organizations like DAV, PVA, VVA, VFW, and
American Legion, et al.

COMMON FORMS

Form 21-22
Appointment of Individual as Claimant's Representative
Form used to document that the veteran is represented by
an advocate.

Form 9 - Appeal to BVA
Also called VA-9 or I-9. Generally must be filed within sixty days
of SOC to perfect substantive appeal.

Form 10-5345
Request for & Authorization to Release Medical Records
Form you use to get VA medical records.

Form 21-526
Original Claim for Compensation or Pension
Only one of these needs to be filed. It will usually support any
subsequent claims or actions.

Form 21-534
Claim for Dependency & Indemnity Compensation
Filed for widow's/survivor's benefits. If a dependent files within a
year after the veteran's death, then the effective date will be the
date of death rather than date of filing.

Form 21-4138
Statement in Support of Claim (SSC/SiSC)
Usually referred to as a 4138. Used for lay statements, NODs,
new claims, reopening requests, etc.

Form 21-4142
Authorization & Consent to Release Information to DVA
Basic release and consent form.

Form 21-8940
Application for Increased Compensation Based on
Unemployability
To file for TDIU. This is considered a claim for increased rating.
You don't need to use the form to let them know that you want
TDIU, but it's easier for them to process. Plus, they will not grant
the claim until they have it.

Form SF-180
For requesting military records
Get it from NPRC website. Look at page 3 of it to see where to
fax or mail it.

Form 3288
Request For and Consent to Release of Information from
Individual's Records
To obtain copy of C-file, or information therein

Form 21-0958
Required NOD form to file appeal to a Rating Decision

COMMON MEDICAL ABBREVIATIONS

ALS   Amyotrophic Lateral Sclerosis (Lou Gehrig's disease)
        Any qualified veteran with this diagnosis is now
        automatically service connected for it, no matter when
        it was diagnosed.

ADLs   Activities of Daily Living
        Occupational therapy assessments describe veteran's
        ability to take care of him/herself.

CC   Chief Complaint
        Medical complaints.

COPD   Chronic Obstructive Pulmonary Disease
        Often caused by asbestos, fumes, or chemical
        exposure.

DDD   Degenerative Disc Disease

DJD   Degenerative Joint Disease

DSM-IV Diagnostic & Statistical Manual (of Mental Disorders),
        4th Ed. Assists in diagnosing psychiatric conditions and
        used in conjunction with rating schedule to assign
        degrees of disability to PTSD and other mental
        conditions. A new manual was released in
        2013: DSM-V.

DX   Diagnosis

EtOH   Alcohol
This is noted both in service records and VA records.

F/U   Follow-Up

GSW   Gunshot Wound
Consider all aspects of the injury—bone, muscle, nerves, scarring.

HX   History

LBP   Low Back Pain
Pain alone isn't compensable, but it may indicate an underlying secondary condition.

LOC   Loss of Consciousness
Mostly associated with TBI. A veteran may still have a substantial concussion without LOC.

MG   Muscle Group

NOS   Not Otherwise Specified
Often seen with mental diagnoses that can't be pinpointed to a specific disorder.

PULHES Physical capacity/stamina, Upper extremities, Lower extremities, Hearing, Eyes, & S psychiatric

Often noted on entrance and separation exams.
Measurement of soldier's overall health.

RA   Rheumatoid Arthritis
Often seen in Gulf War Syndrome cases.

R/O   Rule Out
Some conditions may look like a diagnosis when they
are really just instructions to rule them out.

ROM   Range of Motion
What the VA ratings schedule bases most orthopedic
conditions on. Testing required to be done with a
goniometer.

SFW   Shell Fragment Wound
Often call shrapnel wounds.

SX   Symptoms

WNL   Within Normal Limits
Used for describing virtually any condition that appears
normal on exam.

COMMON QUESTIONS

1. What is the C-file?

The file the VA benefits section keeps on your claims. It should have all information on any and every claim you have filed since discharge. This file is different from the file that the VA health section keeps on you. It is important to obtain your C-file to make sure the VA has all the evidence you submitted and all the evidence it told you it would obtain for your claim.

2. What is a C&P exam and do I have to go?

The C&P exam is set up by the VA benefits section. Generally, it will not be conducted by your treating VA doctor. The purpose of the exam is to determine if your disability is service connected and/or to determine the severity of the disability. You must attend this exam, even if you have strong supporting evidence from other VA doctors or private doctors. If you do not attend the exam, then the VA can automatically deny your claim.

3. How far back can my benefits go?

Benefits typically go back to the date you filed your current claim. There are some exceptions though.

4. If I'm approved, how do I get paid?

The VA prefers to pay through electronic deposit, meaning that it directly deposits the money into your bank account.

5. Can the VA ever reduce my benefits?

Yes, the VA can reduce benefits, but only in certain cases, and only when specific legal requirements are met. There are some instances in which a rating, or even a disability's status as service connected, is protected. For instance, total/100% ratings (including TDIU determinations), or ratings that have been in effect for five years or more, are afforded special protection. Likewise, those disabilities that have been rated at or above a particular rating level for twenty years or more cannot be reduced below that level unless the VA determines the rating was based on fraud.

6. Will my family continue to get benefits when I die?

Not automatically. Dependents will not receive the benefits that the veteran received when he was living. But the dependents can apply for a death pension, which is income based, and/or Dependency & Indemnity Compensation (DIC), which is based on the veteran's death being related to a service connected disability or the veteran being rated at 100% for a certain amount of time.

7. Why should I hire an attorney?

We recommend that you apply for benefits first with a VSO or by yourself. The VA must help you with your VA claim. If you receive a decision with which you disagree, then consider hiring an attorney. An attorney can typically offer a more thorough review of your case. An attorney can also provide extra resources to help you, such as finding doctors for outside exams and military historians for record research.

8. What should I look for in an attorney?

An attorney should have more experience with VA law than just being accredited by the VA. This accreditation is no indication of actual experience. Also, an attorney should have VA law as his/her primary or only practice area. VA law is extremely complicated and cannot be practiced well part time. And ideally, an attorney should give presentations or seminars regarding VA law or how to practice VA law, a demonstration of expertise in the field.

9. Can the attorney speed up the appeals process?

No. Any advocate who says he can speed up the process is not telling the truth. As I tell my veteran clients, I have not had much success in getting the VA to act in a timely manner, but I have had great success in getting the VA to make the right decision. There are really only two ways that the veteran can speed up his claim: by showing proof of extreme financial hardship, or by showing that he has a terminal illness. Unfortunately, even these two situations do not guarantee a timely decision.

10. Do I have to dismiss my VSO?

An attorney cannot represent a veteran who is also represented by a VSO, but you do not have to dismiss one representative to hire another. You simply have to file a new VA form 21-22a (Appointment of Individual as Claimant's Representative), and the VA will recognize your new advocate as your representative.

ABOUT THE AUTHORS

Mr. Hill focuses his practice on representing disabled veterans. He represents veterans and their dependents across the nation. He has review over 10,000 claims of veterans going through the VA service connected disability compensation process. Mr. Hill limits his practice to psychiatric cases—especially PTSD—Agent Orange exposure cases, Individual Unemployability, Gulf War Syndrome and other chemical exposure issues.

Mr. Hill is a recognized authority on VA law. He has authored several books on VA service connected benefits. Mr. Hill gives presentations across the nation on VA disability compensation, including the pitfalls of C&P exams. He is the treasurer for the board of directors of the National Organization of Veterans Advocates (NOVA).

Mr. Hill attended the University of Florida and earned his Bachelor of Arts degree in Spanish in 2002. He was elected into Phi Beta Kappa and graduated Cum Laude. He attended law school at the University of Florida and was awarded the book award in Trial Practice. He earned his law Degree in 2005. Before attending the University of Florida, Mr. Hill spent a year in Uruguay where he became fluent in Spanish.

After graduating law school, Mr. Hill was a Judicial Law Clerk to The Honorable Anne C. Conway, U.S. District Court for the Middle District of Florida. While working for Judge Conway, Mr. Hill drafted orders, researched complex legal issues, and attended trials and hearings. Mr. Hill also assisted Judge Conway when she sat by designation with the Eleventh Circuit Court of Appeals in Atlanta, Georgia.

Brenda Duplantis has been helping clients at Hill & Ponton with disability claims since 1991.

Ms. Duplantis earned an Associate in Arts degree from Valencia Community College, Orlando, Florida. She has also studied Industrial Engineering at the University of Central Florida, Orlando, Florida.

She is fluent in Spanish and is an Ambassador for the Hispanic Chamber of Commerce Metro Orlando where she helps promote and ensure membership involvement for chamber advancement.

She is a certified yoga teacher and during her spare time she enjoys volunteering at schools and non-profit organizations teaching and advocating the benefits of Lymphatic Yoga.